Fuck Off Secret

Hilarious Swear Word Coloring Book

For Fun & Stress Releasing

Charles C. Golden

Happy Coloring!

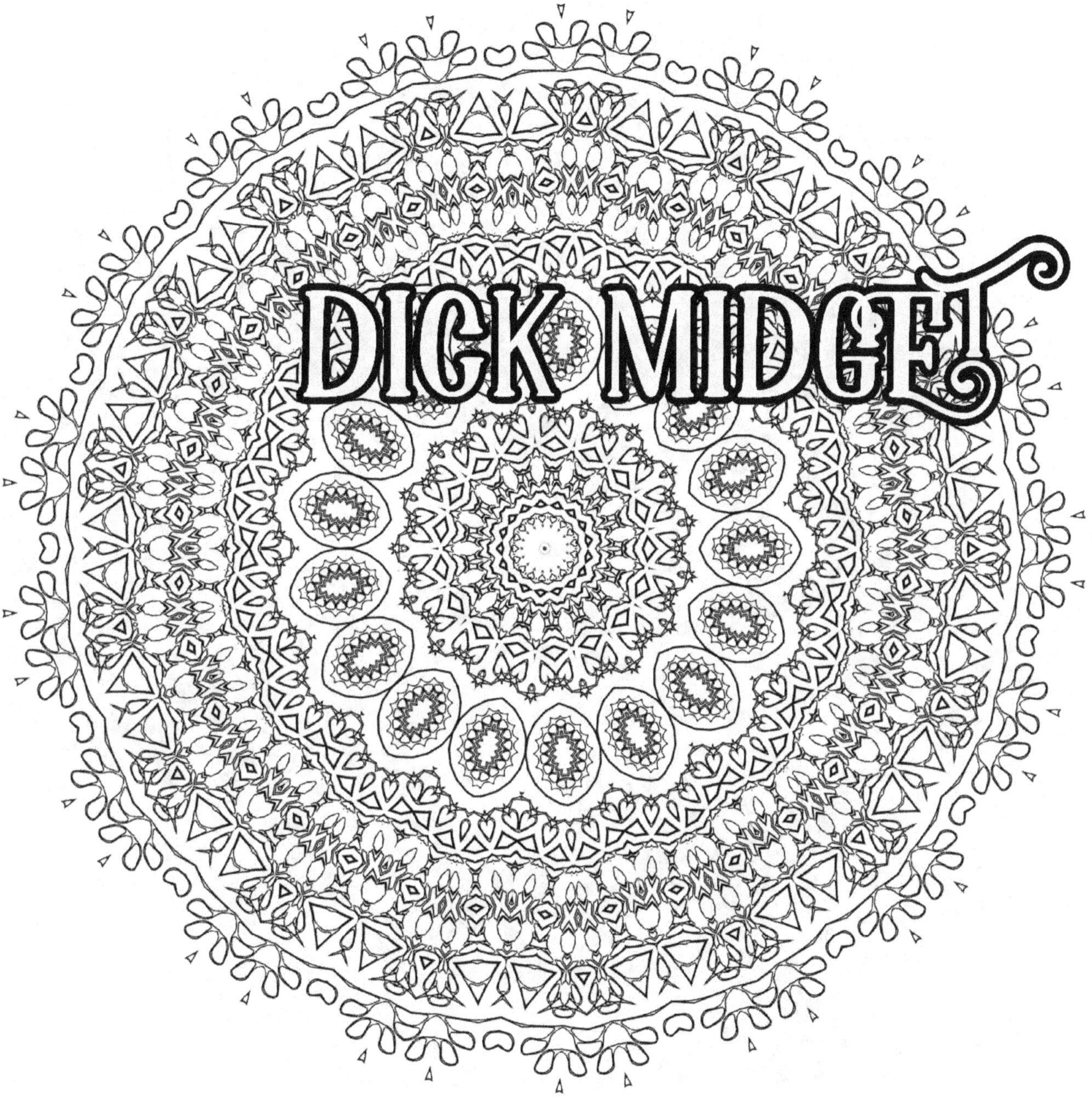
DICK MIDGET

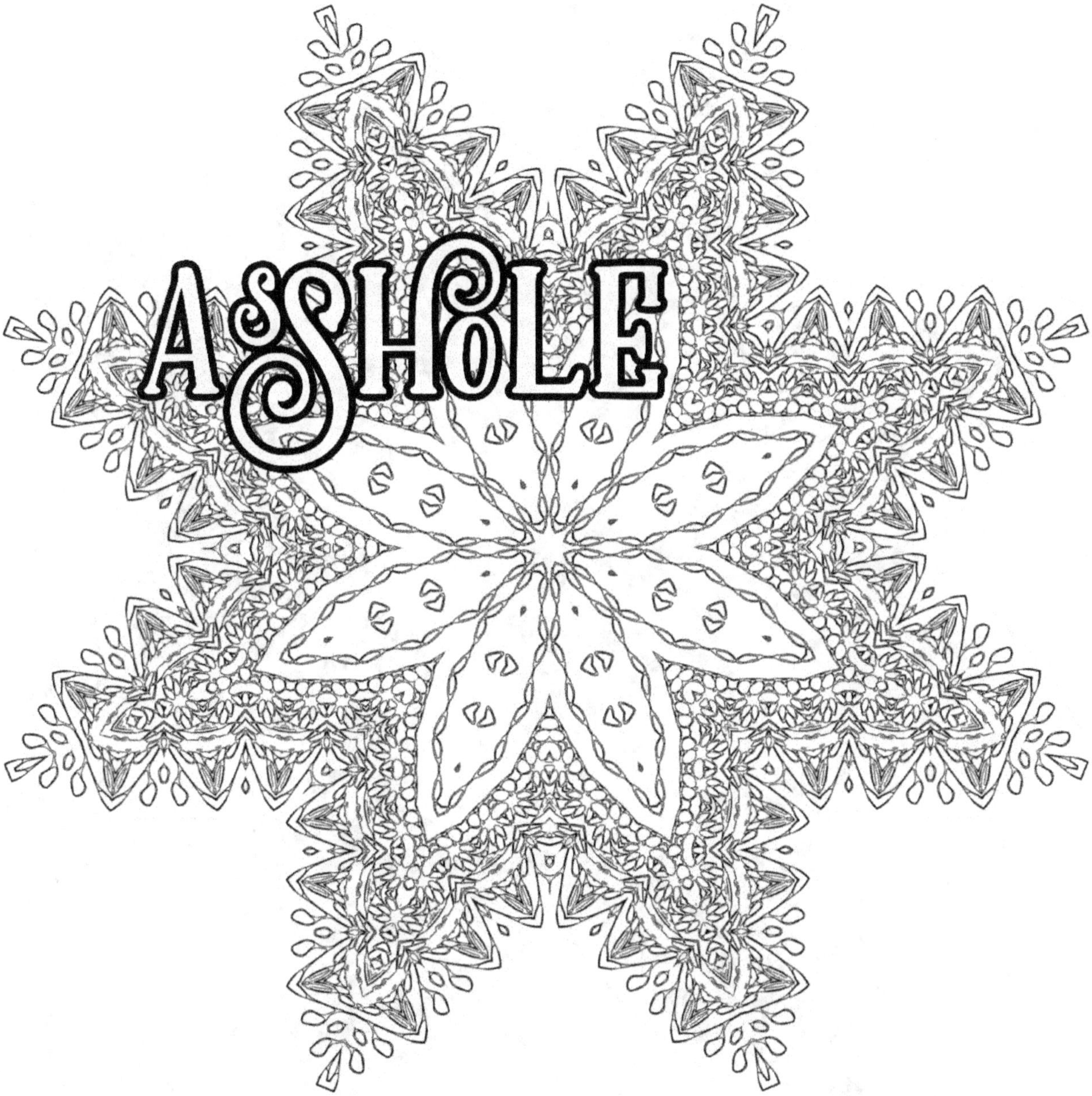
ASSHOLE

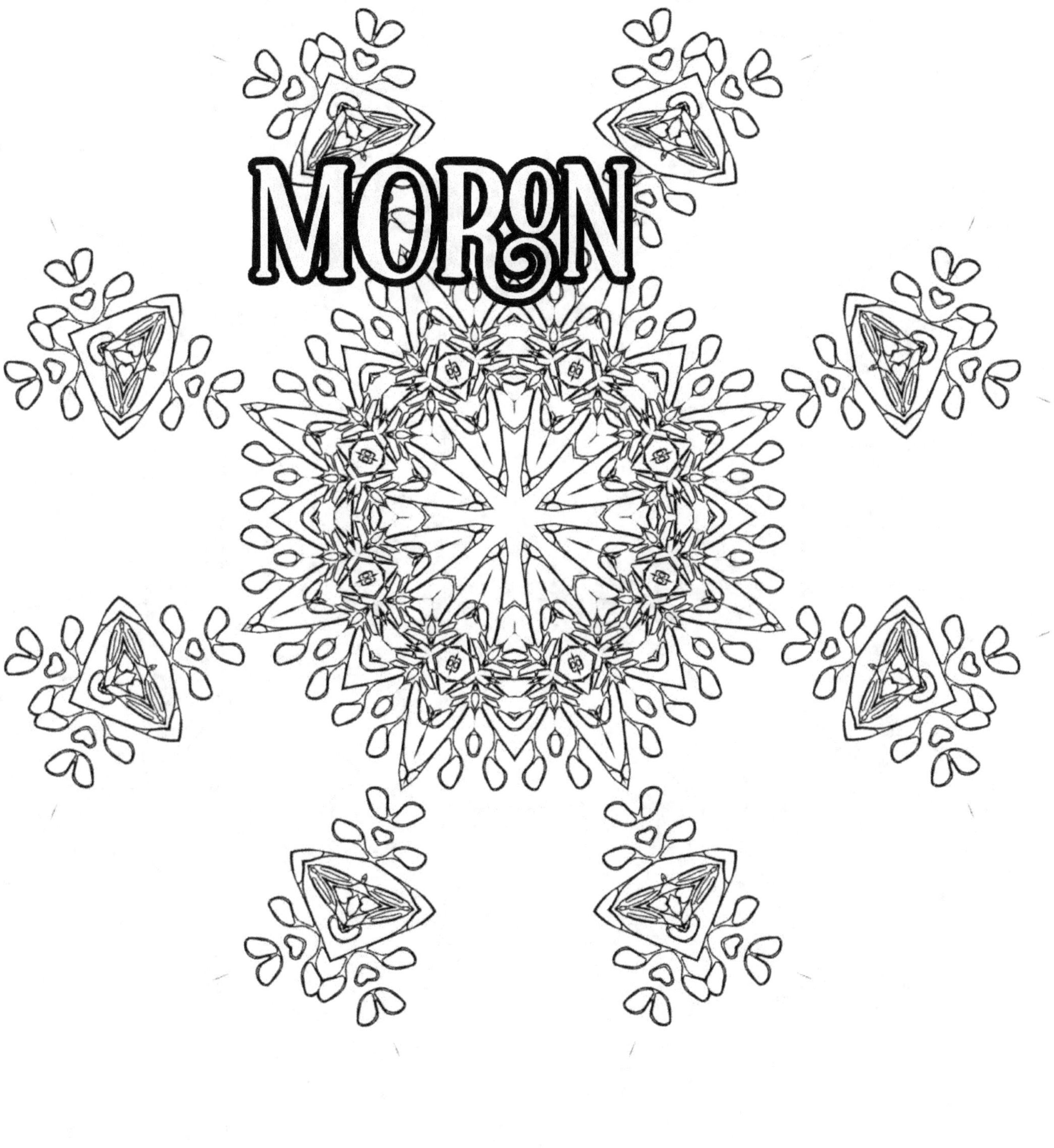
MORON

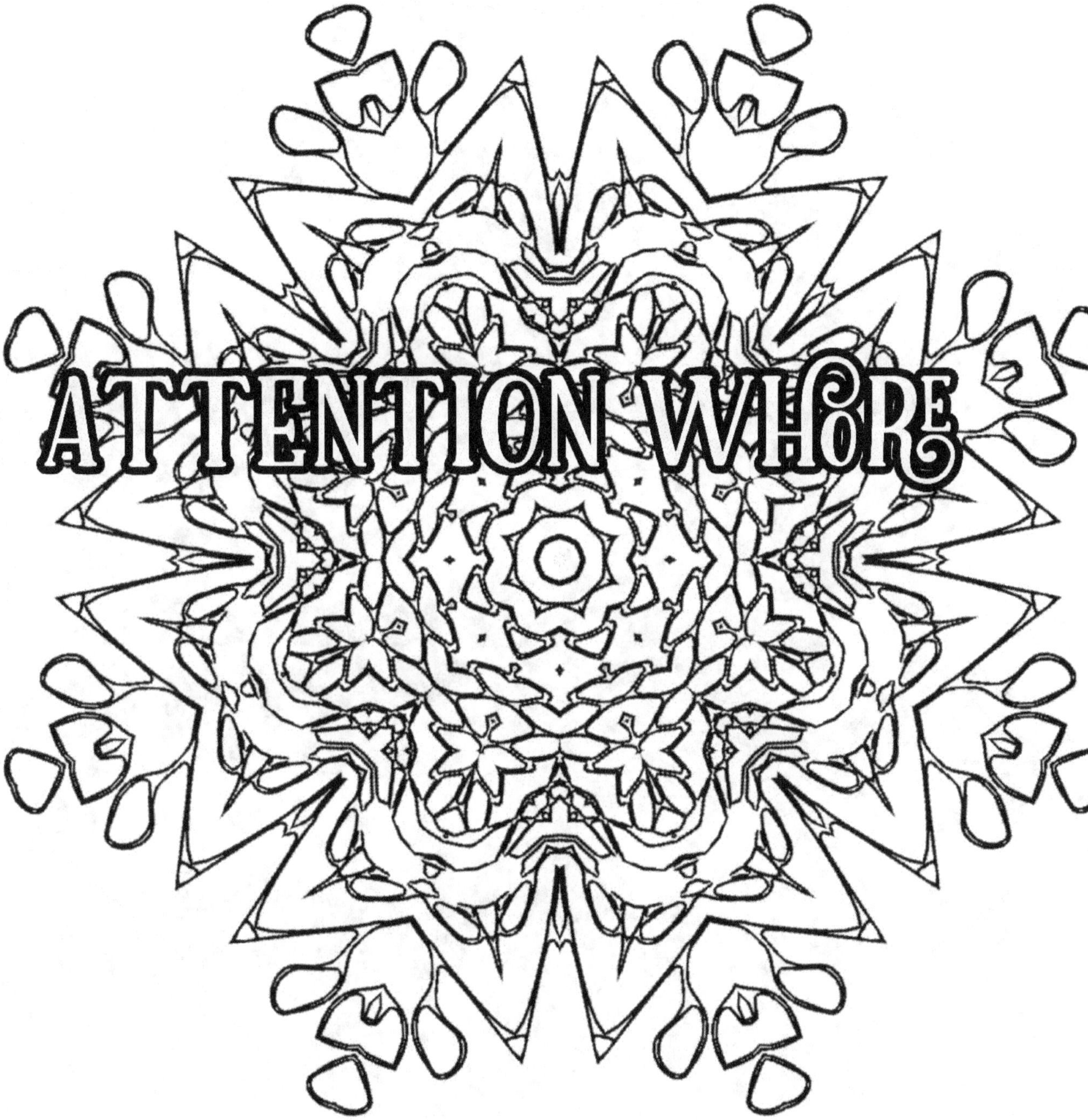
ATTENTION WHORE

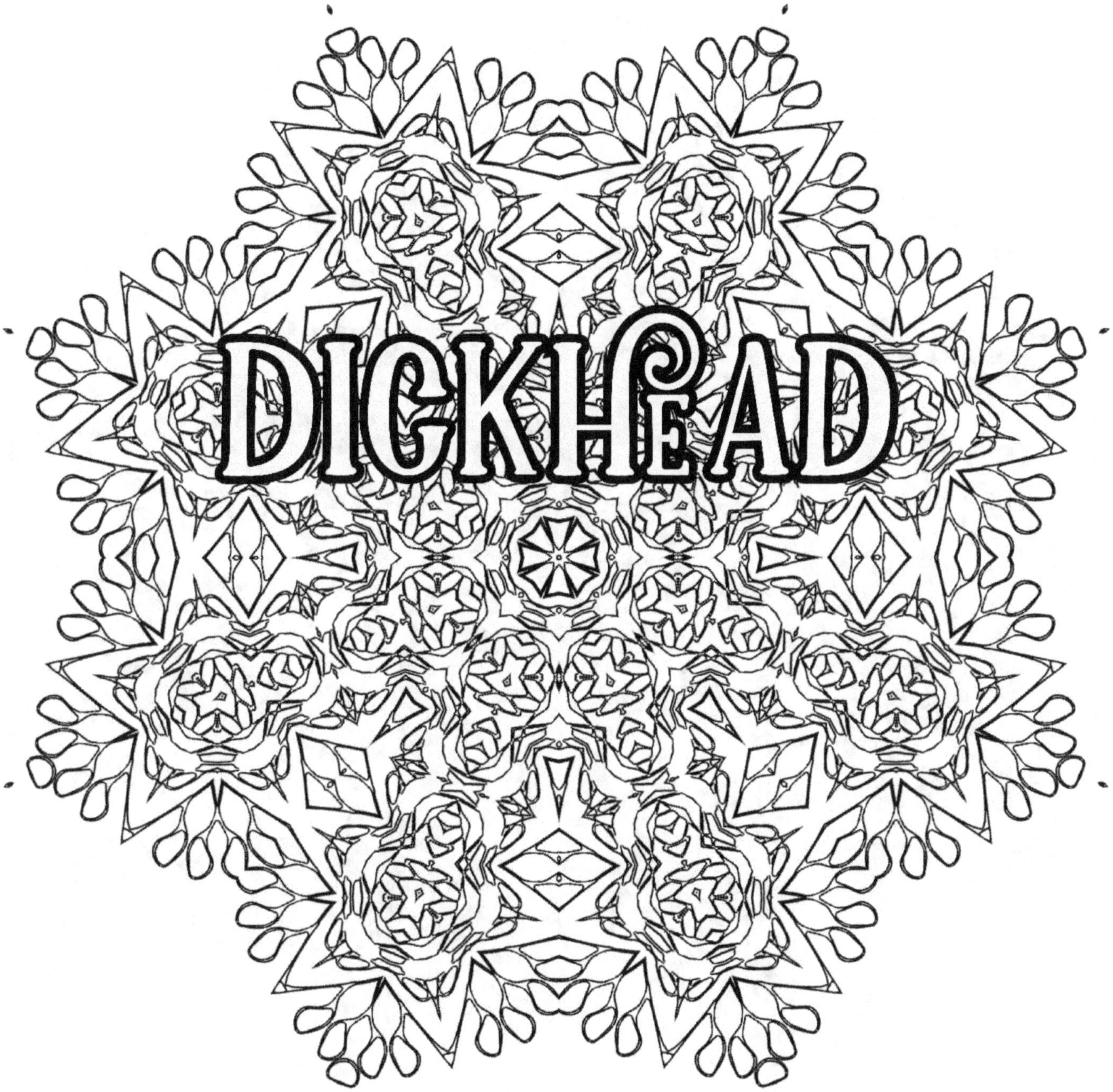
DICKHEAD

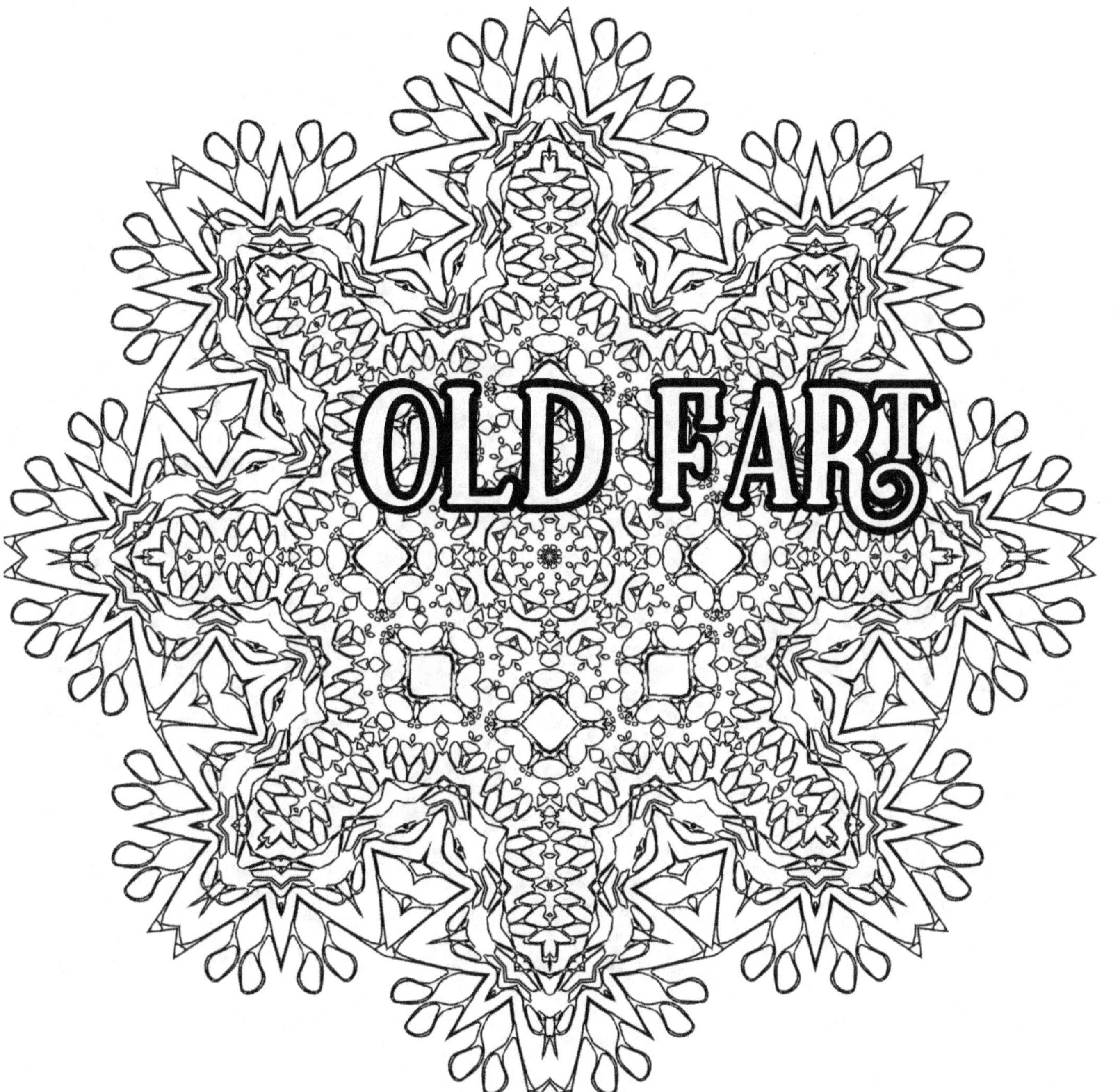
OLD FART

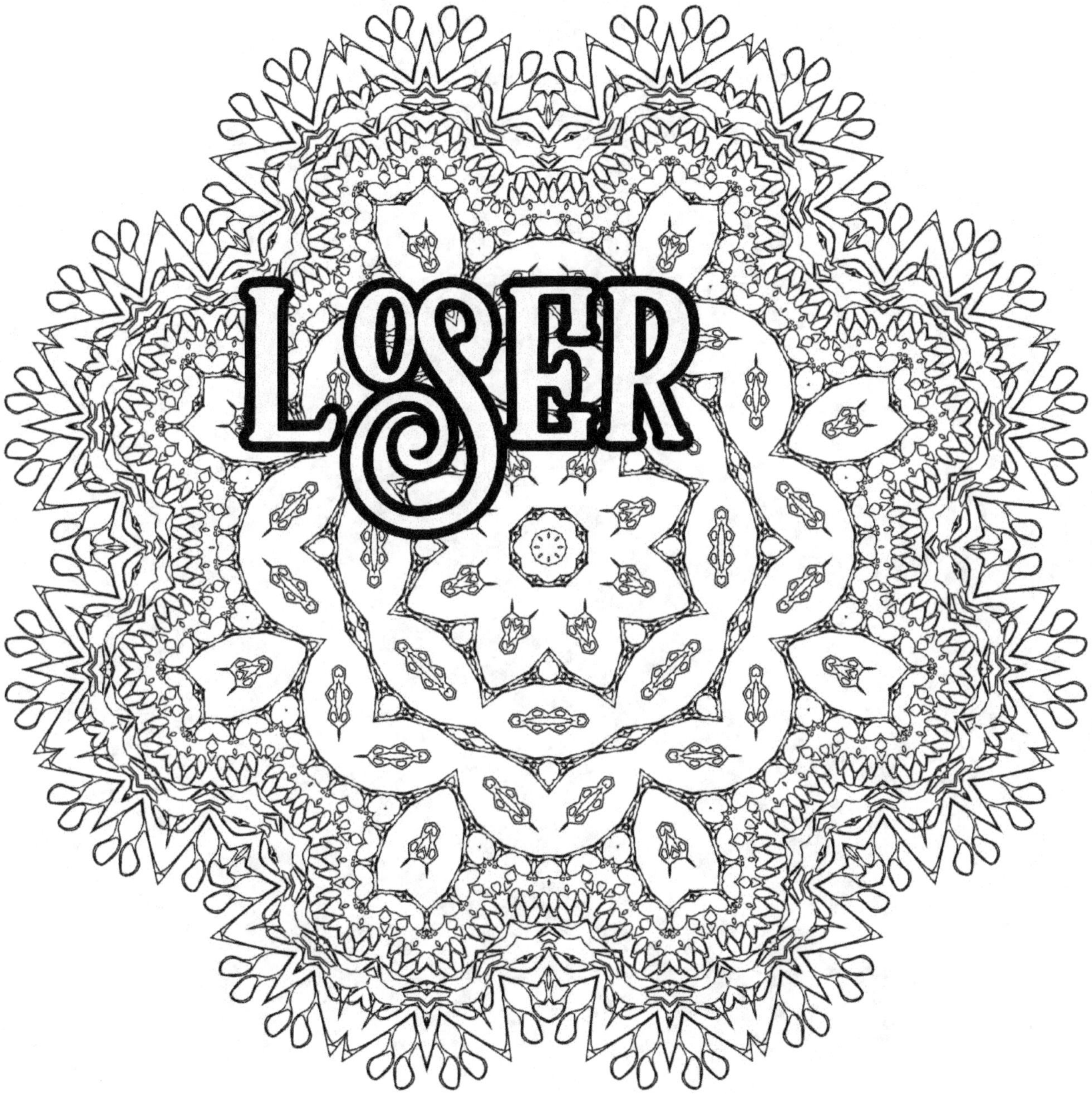
LOSER

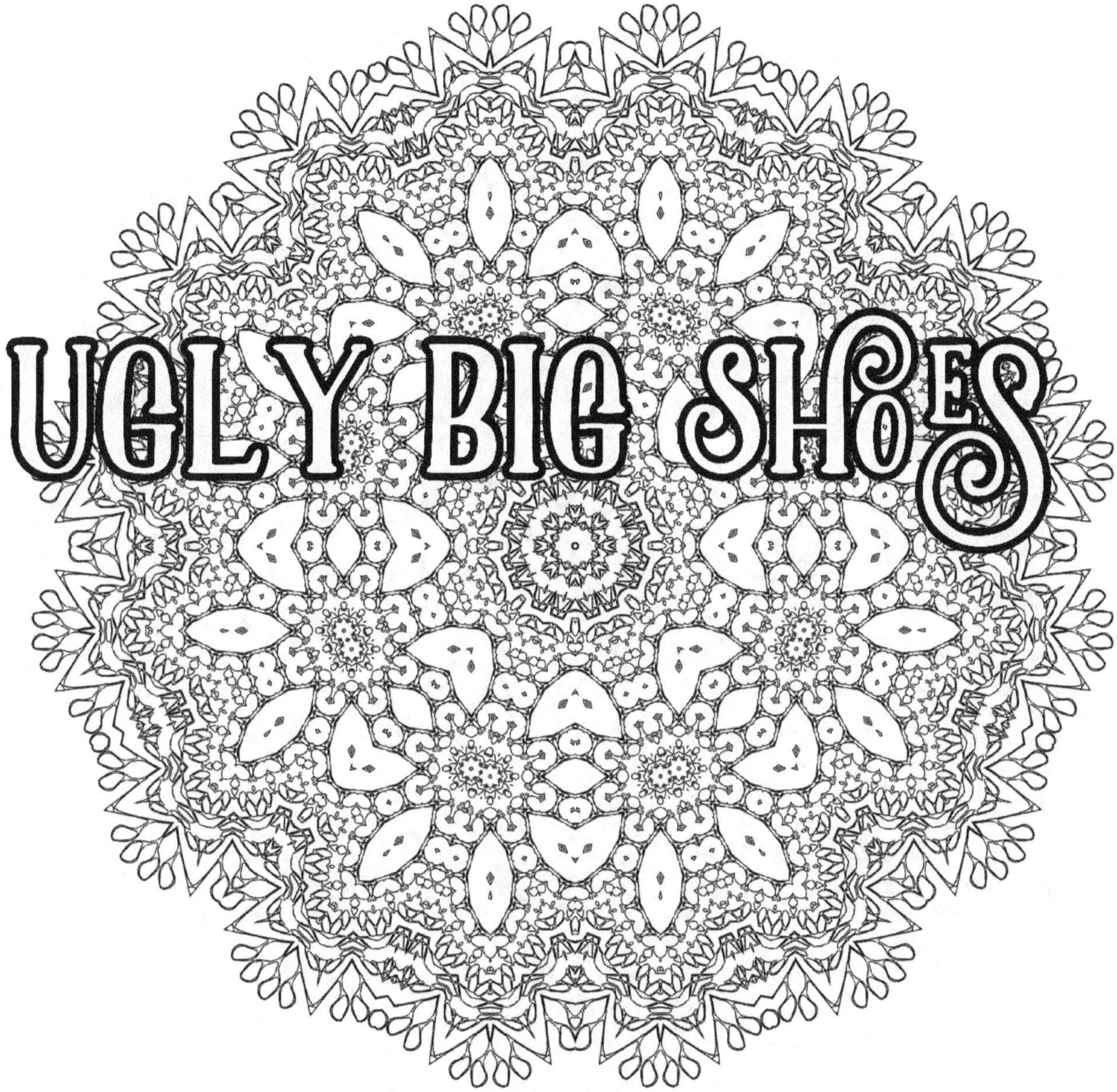
UGLY BIG SHOES

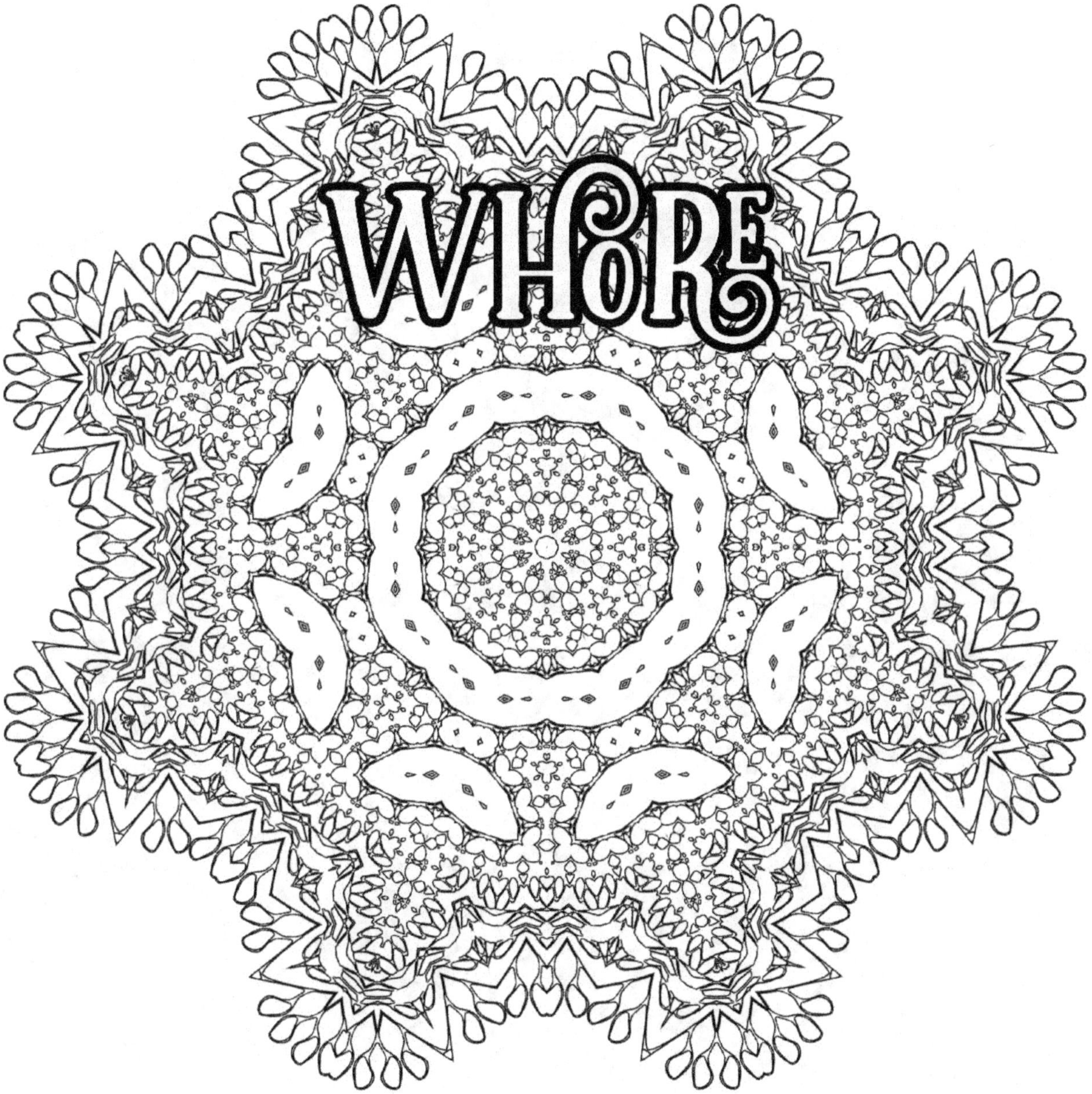
WHORE

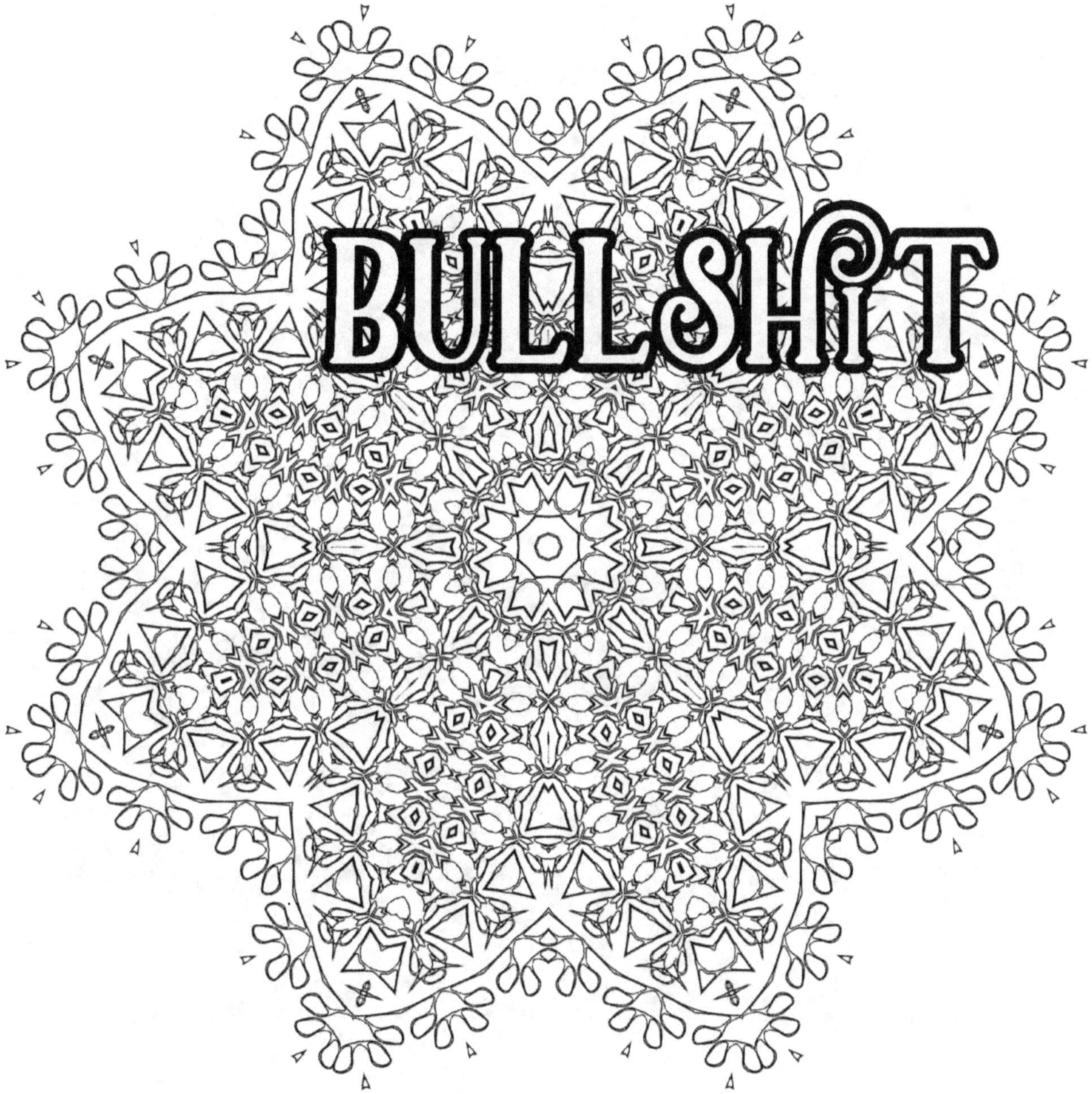
BULLSHiT

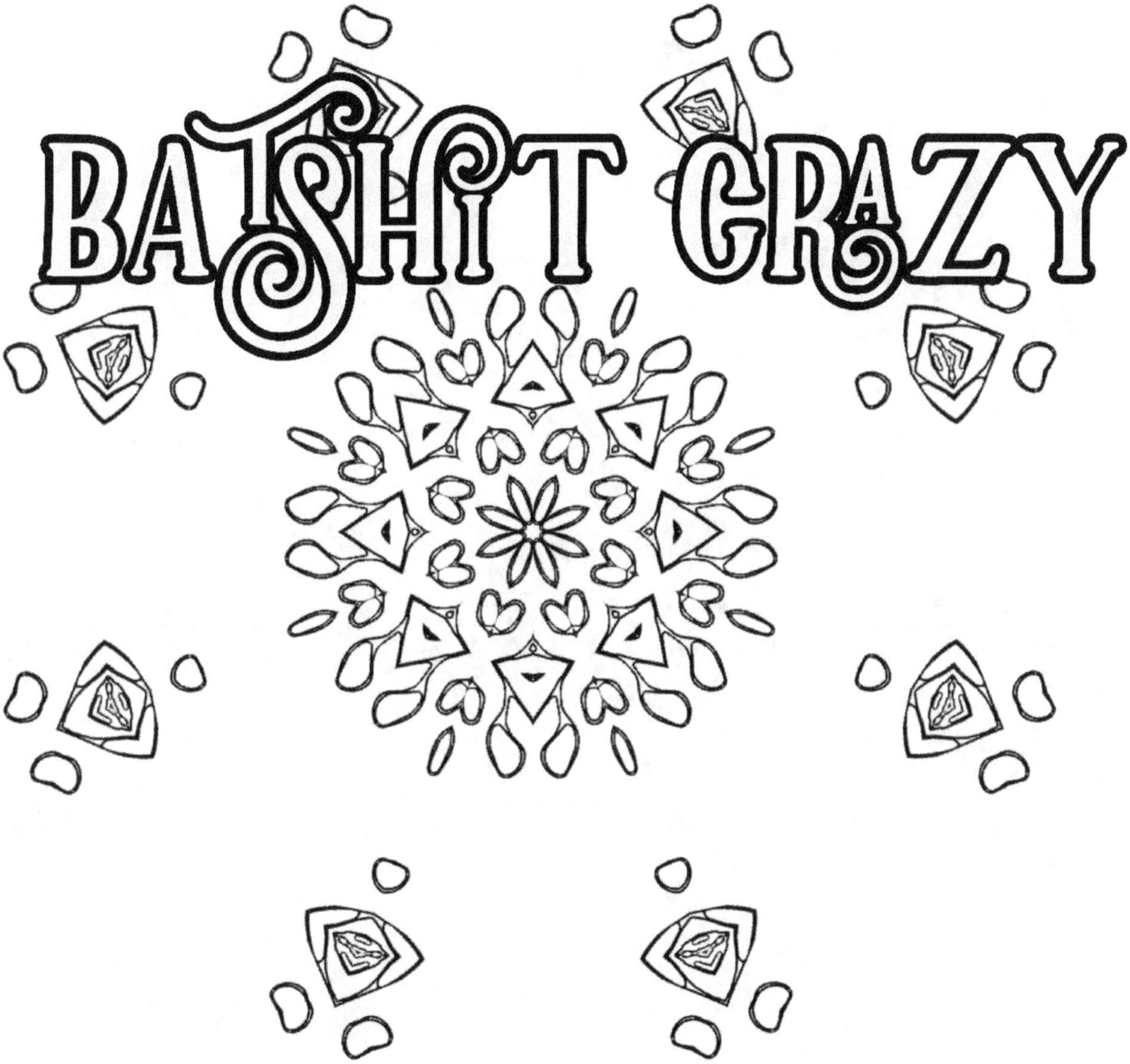
BATSHIT CRAZY

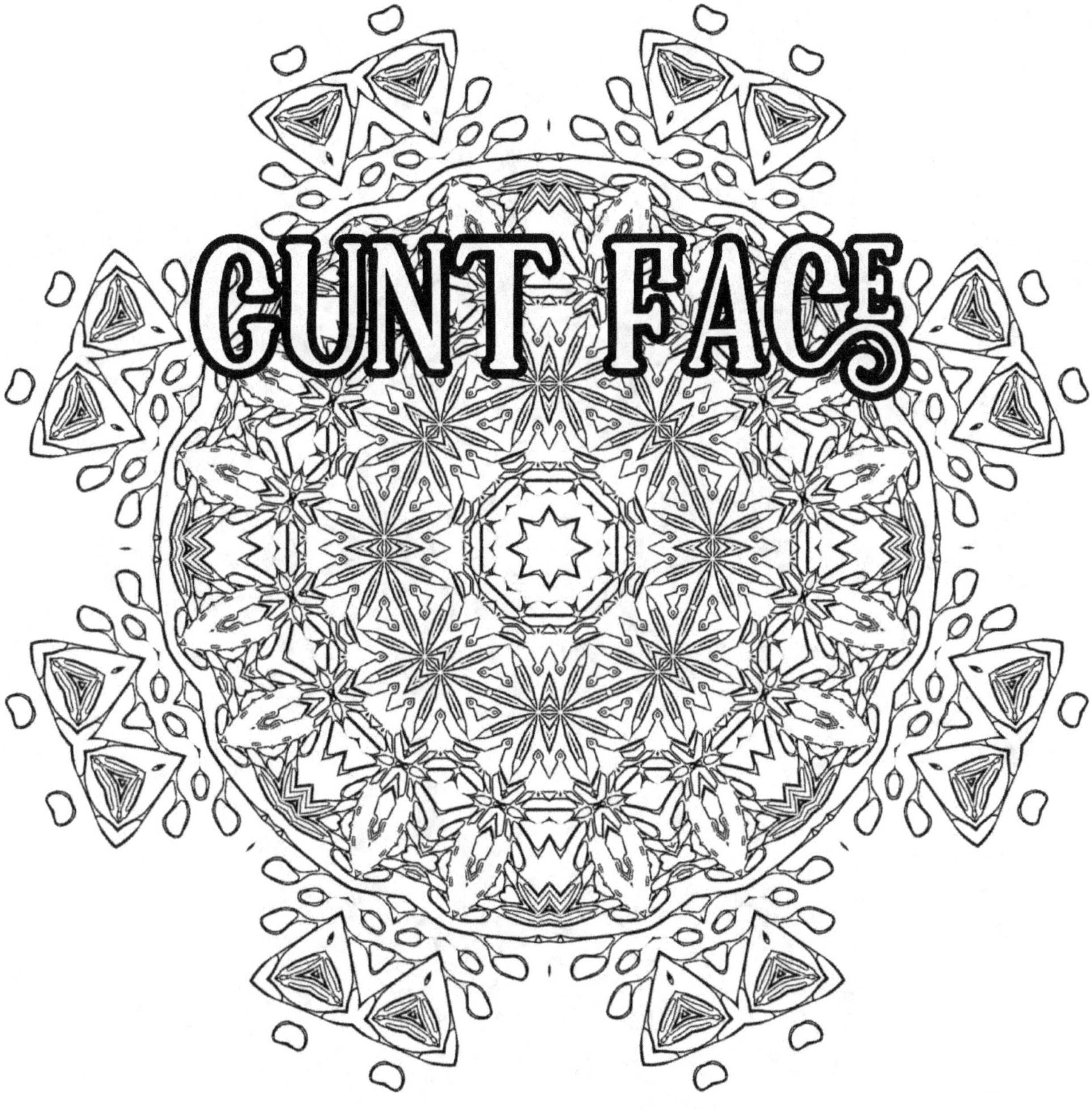
CUNT FACE

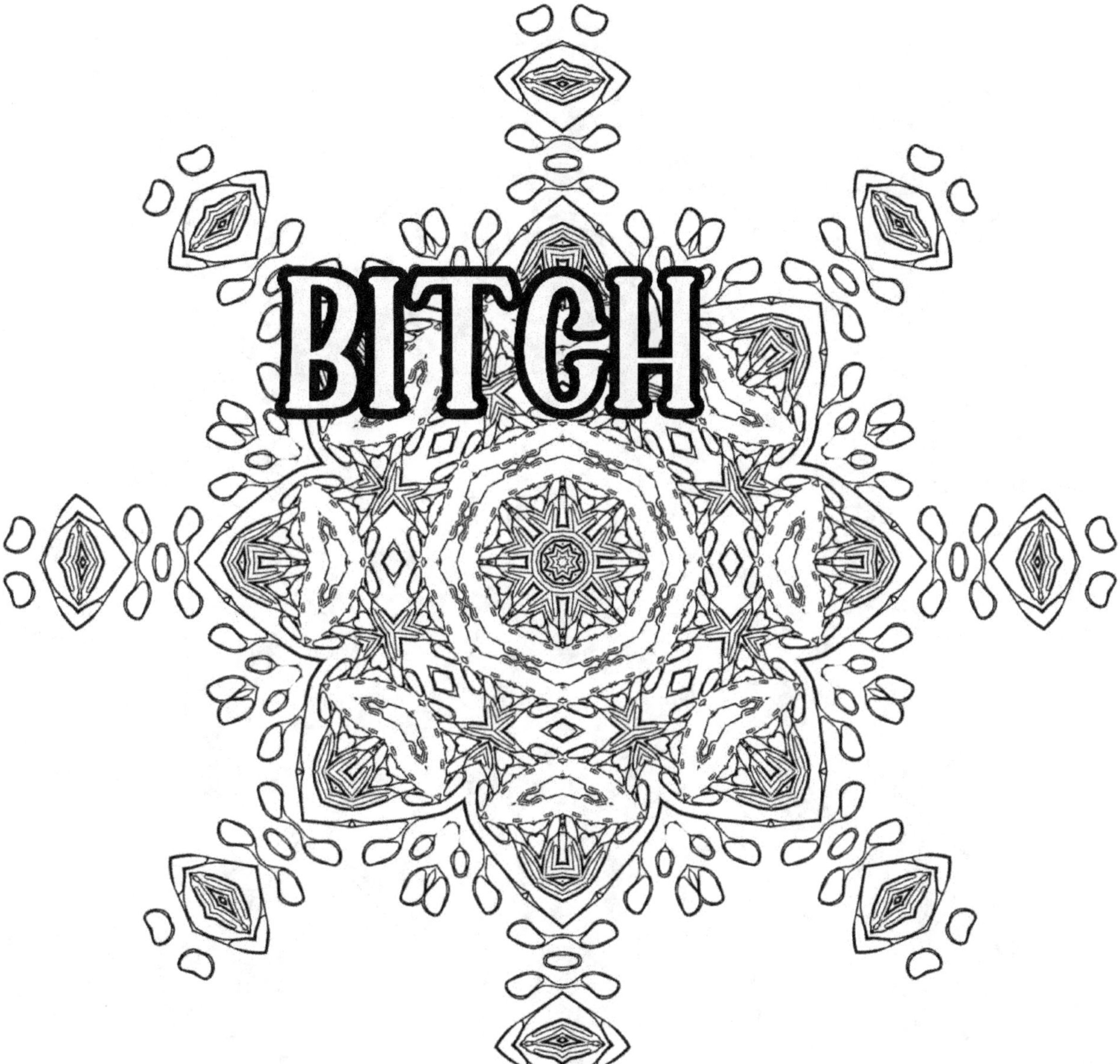
BITCH

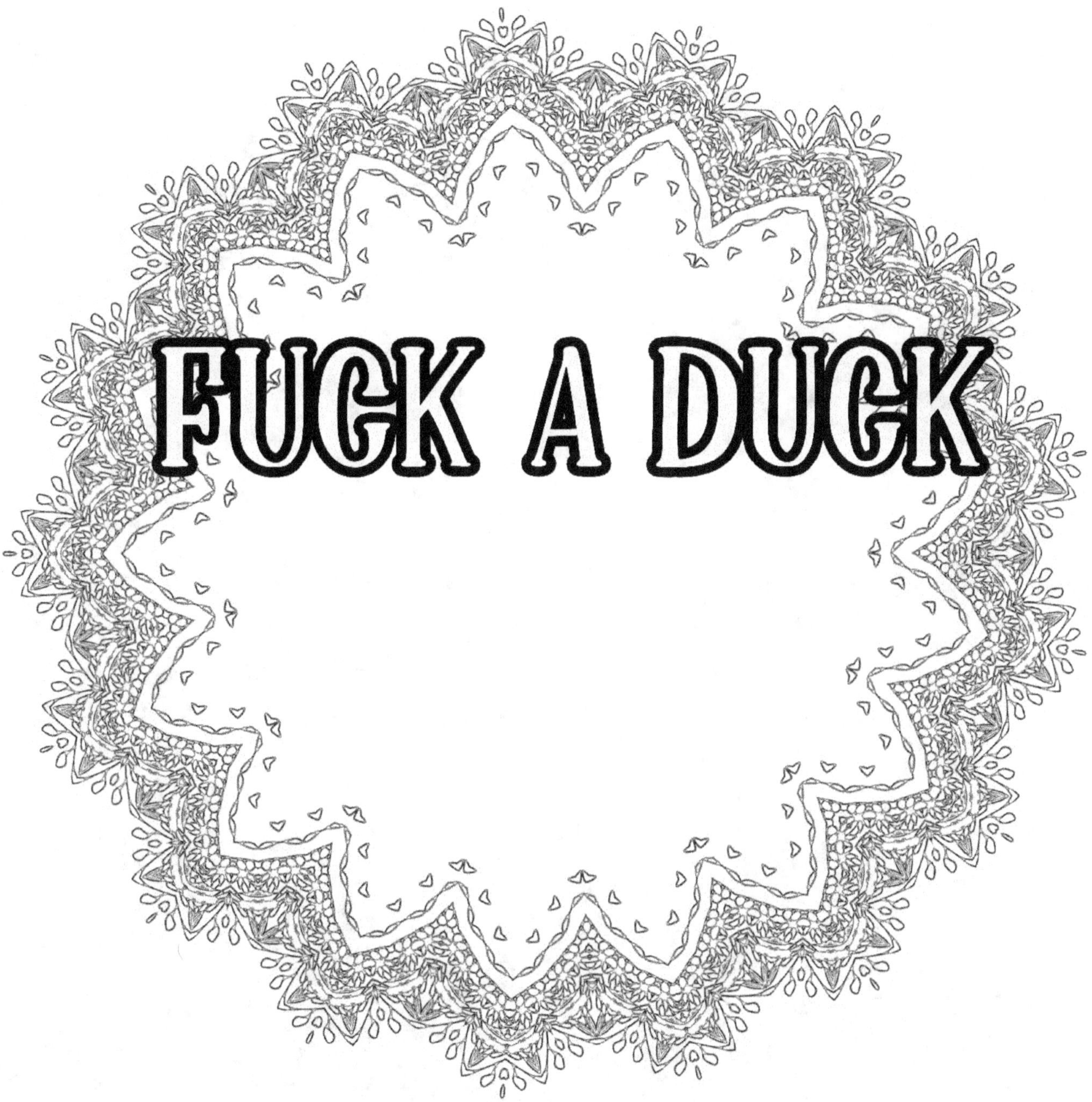
FUCK A DUCK

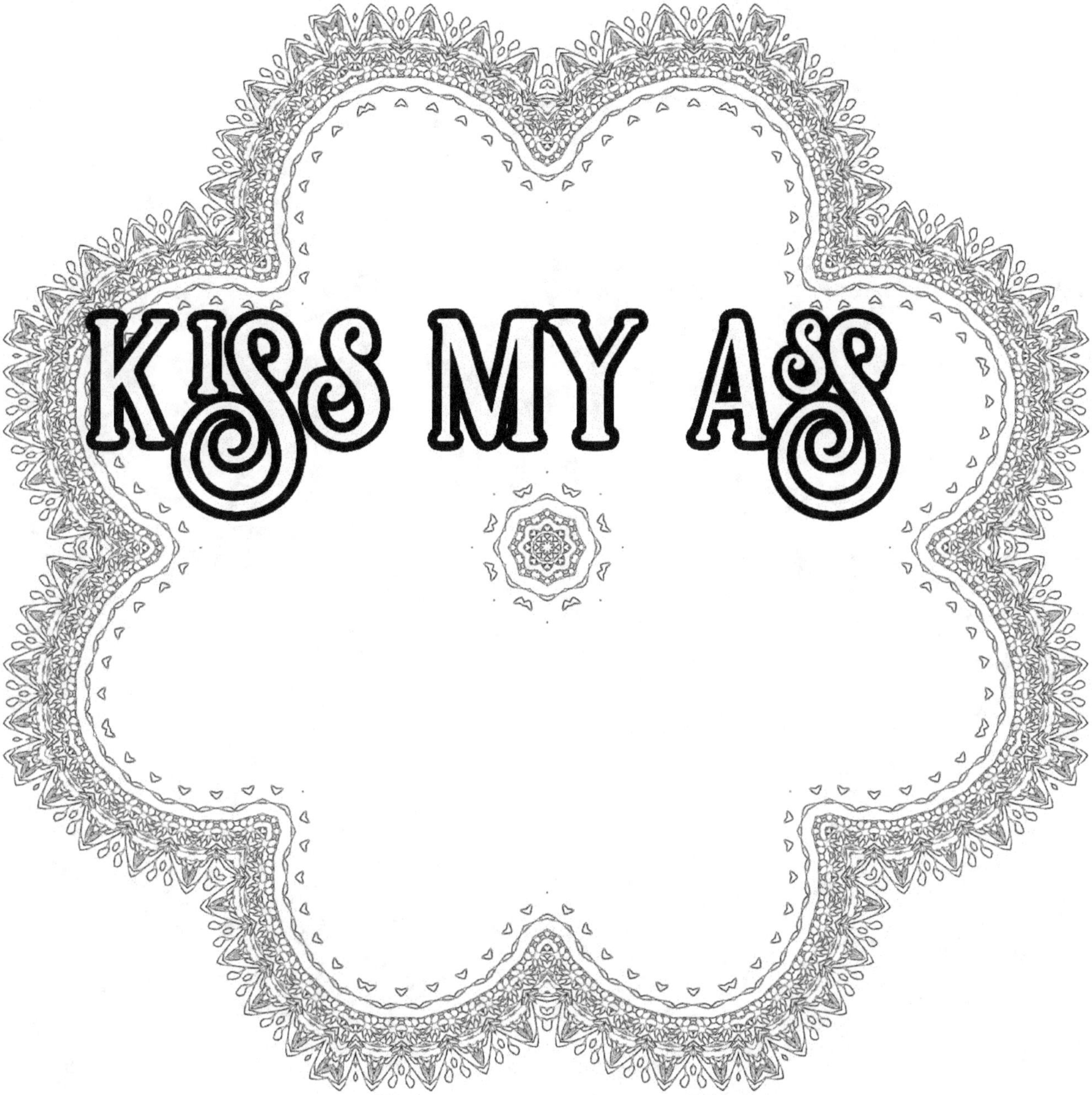
KISS MY ASS

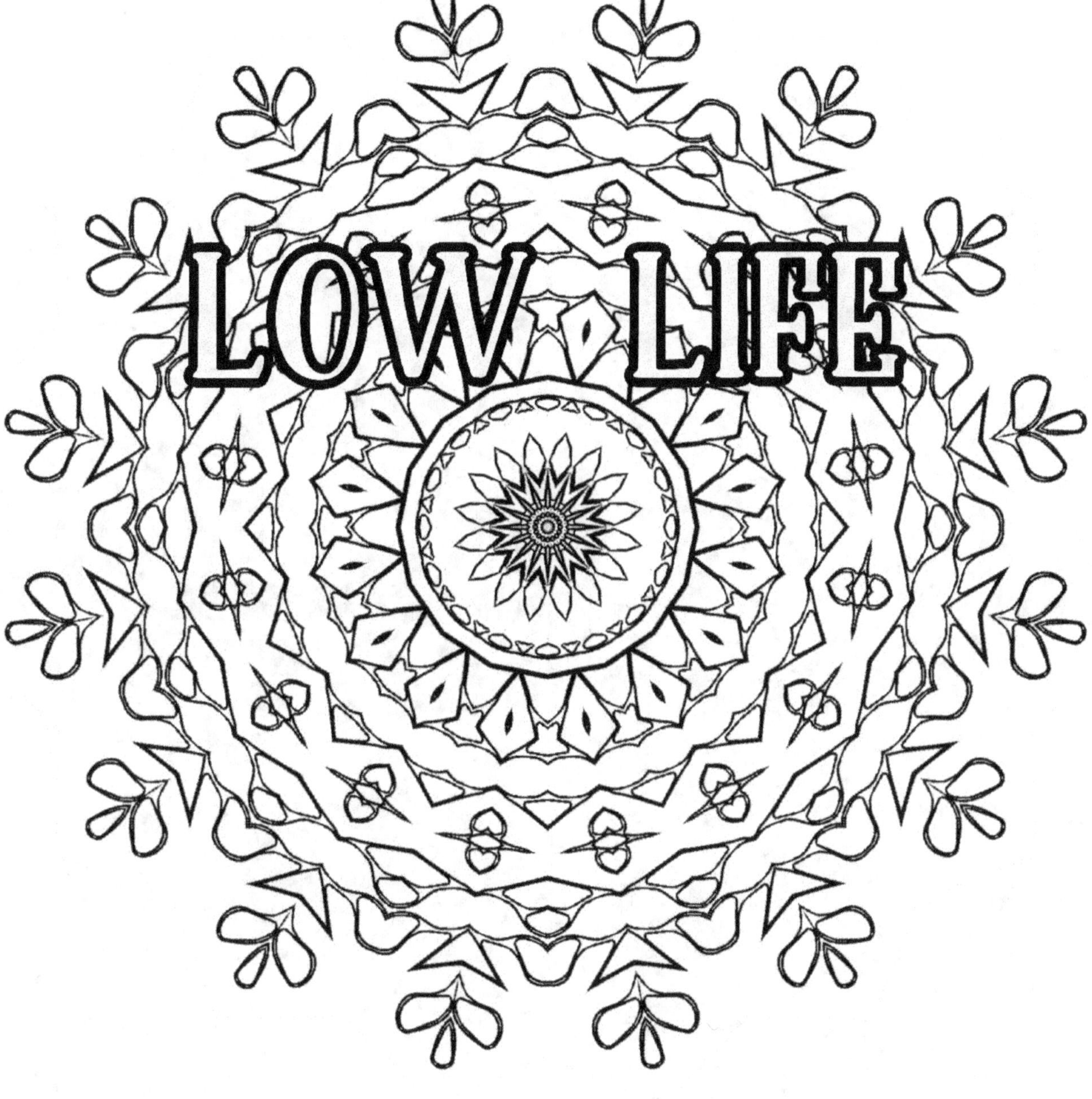
LOW LIFE

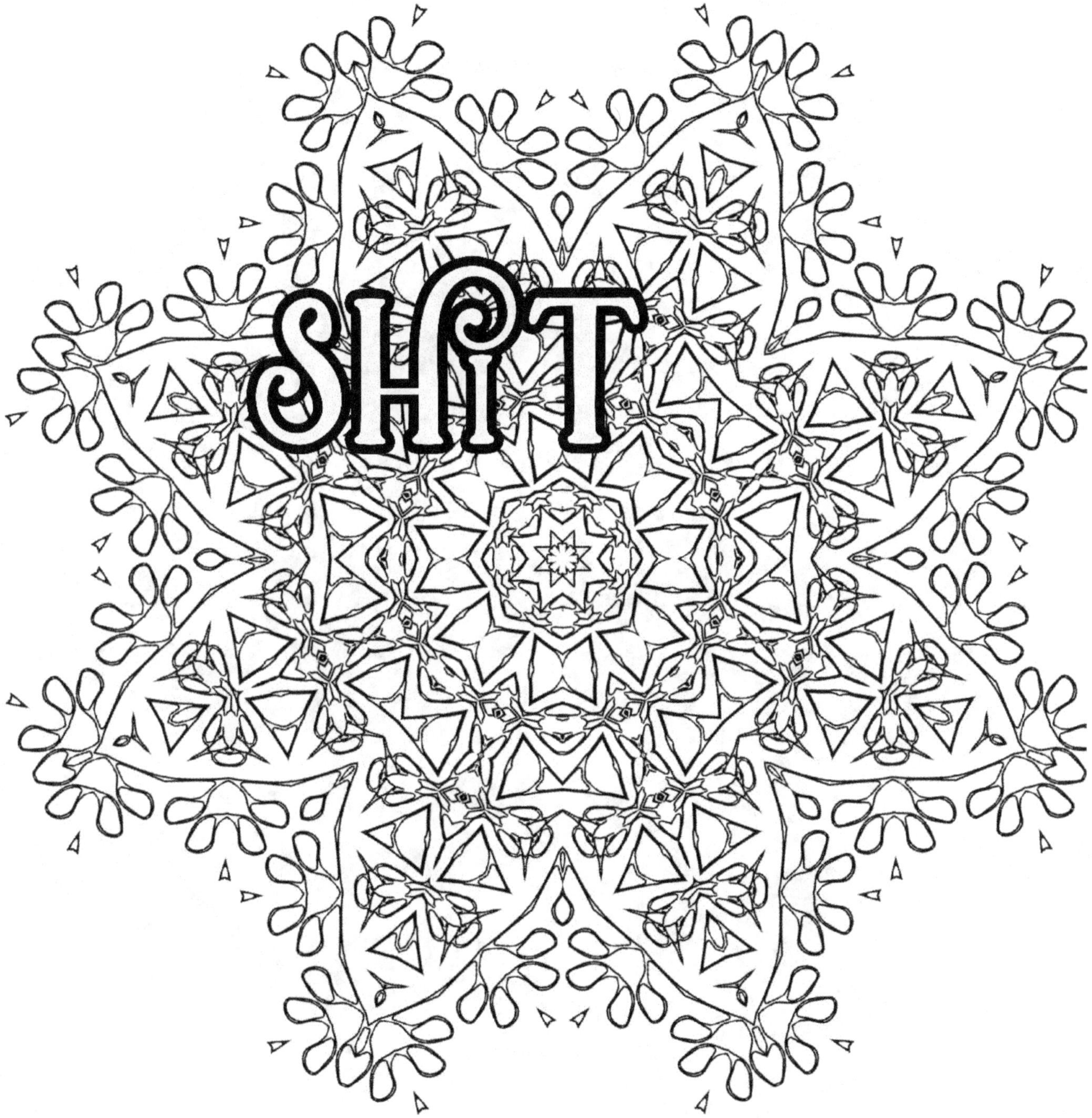
SHIT

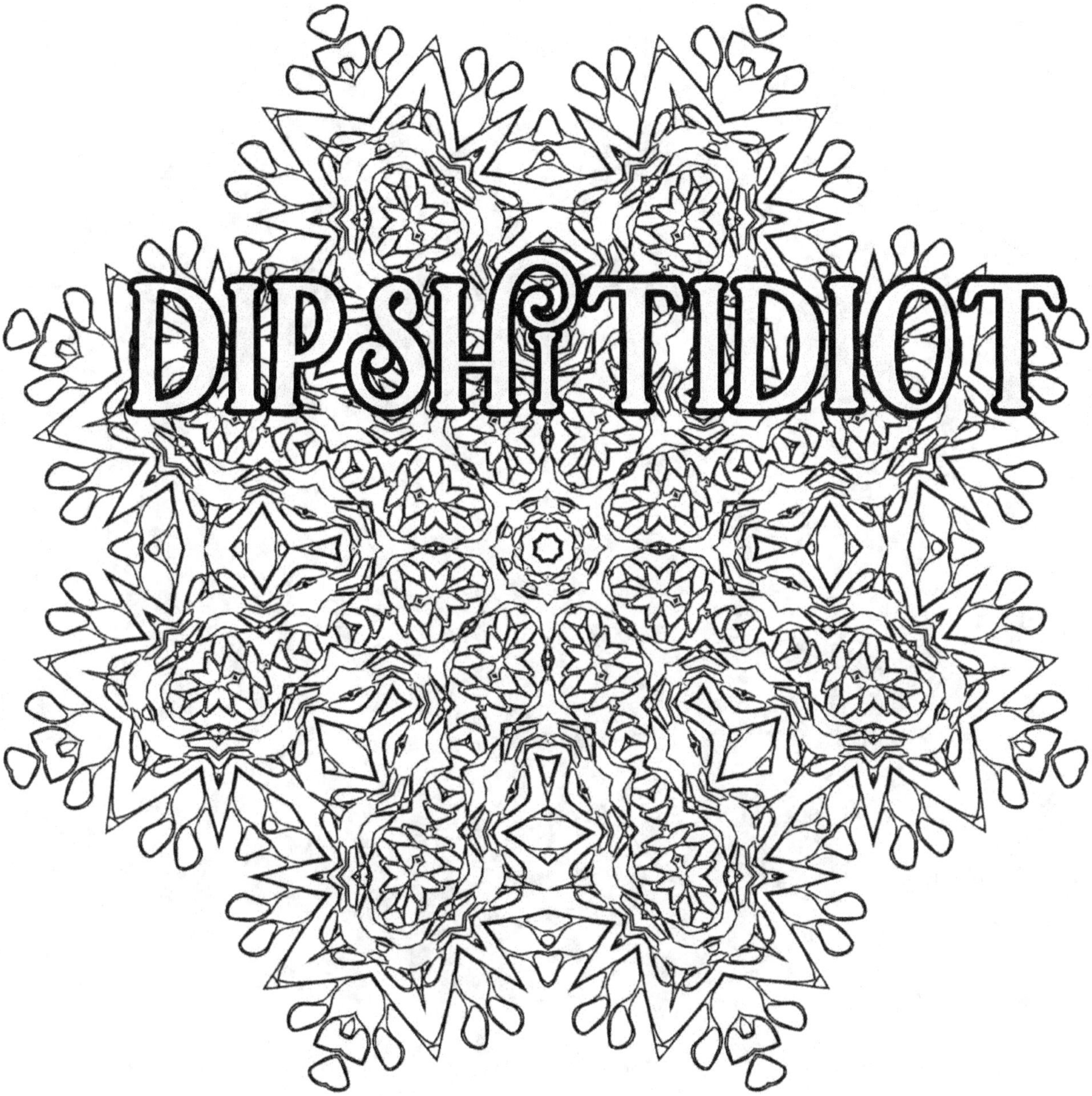
DIPSHIT IDIOT

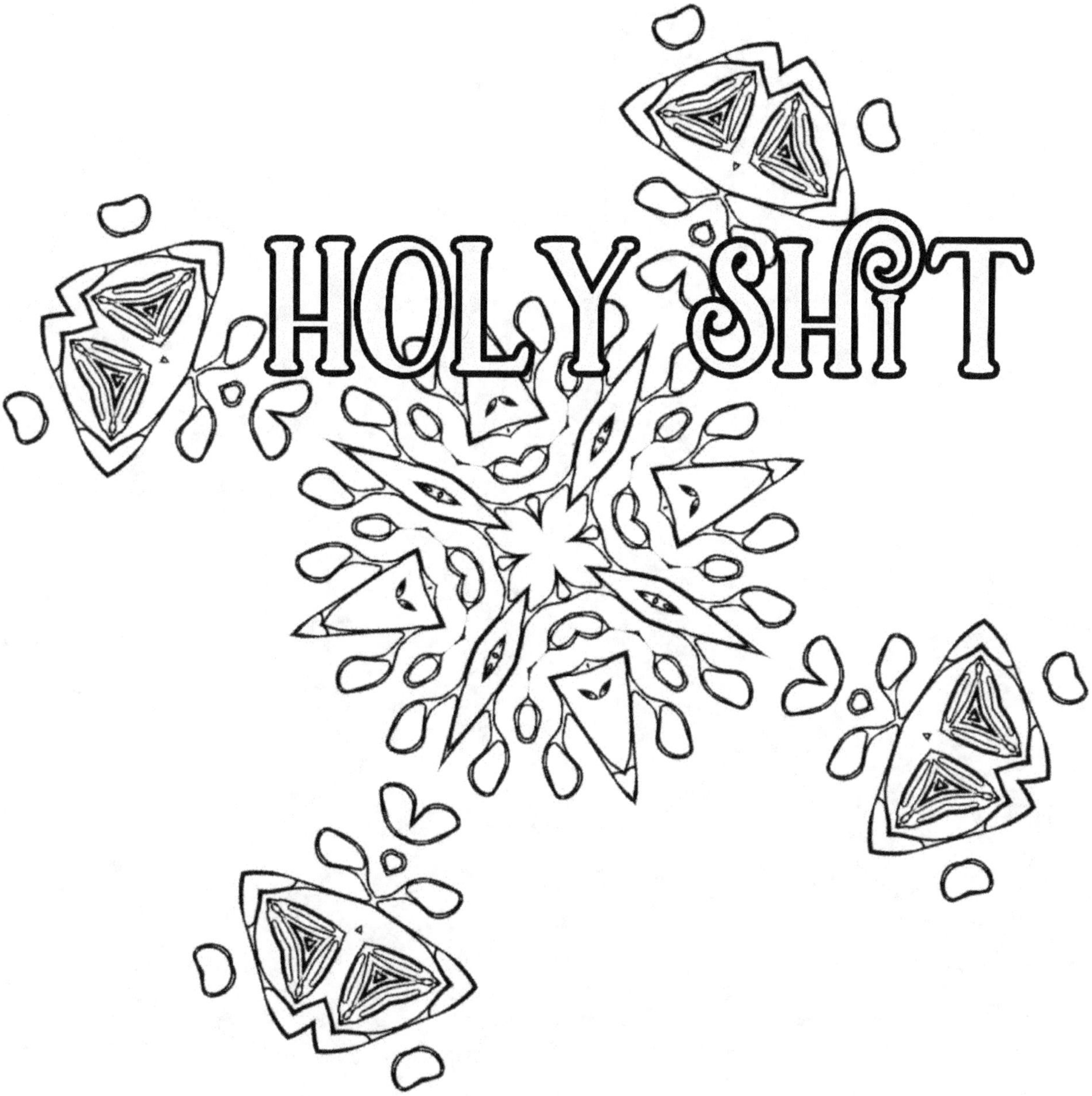
HOLY SHIT

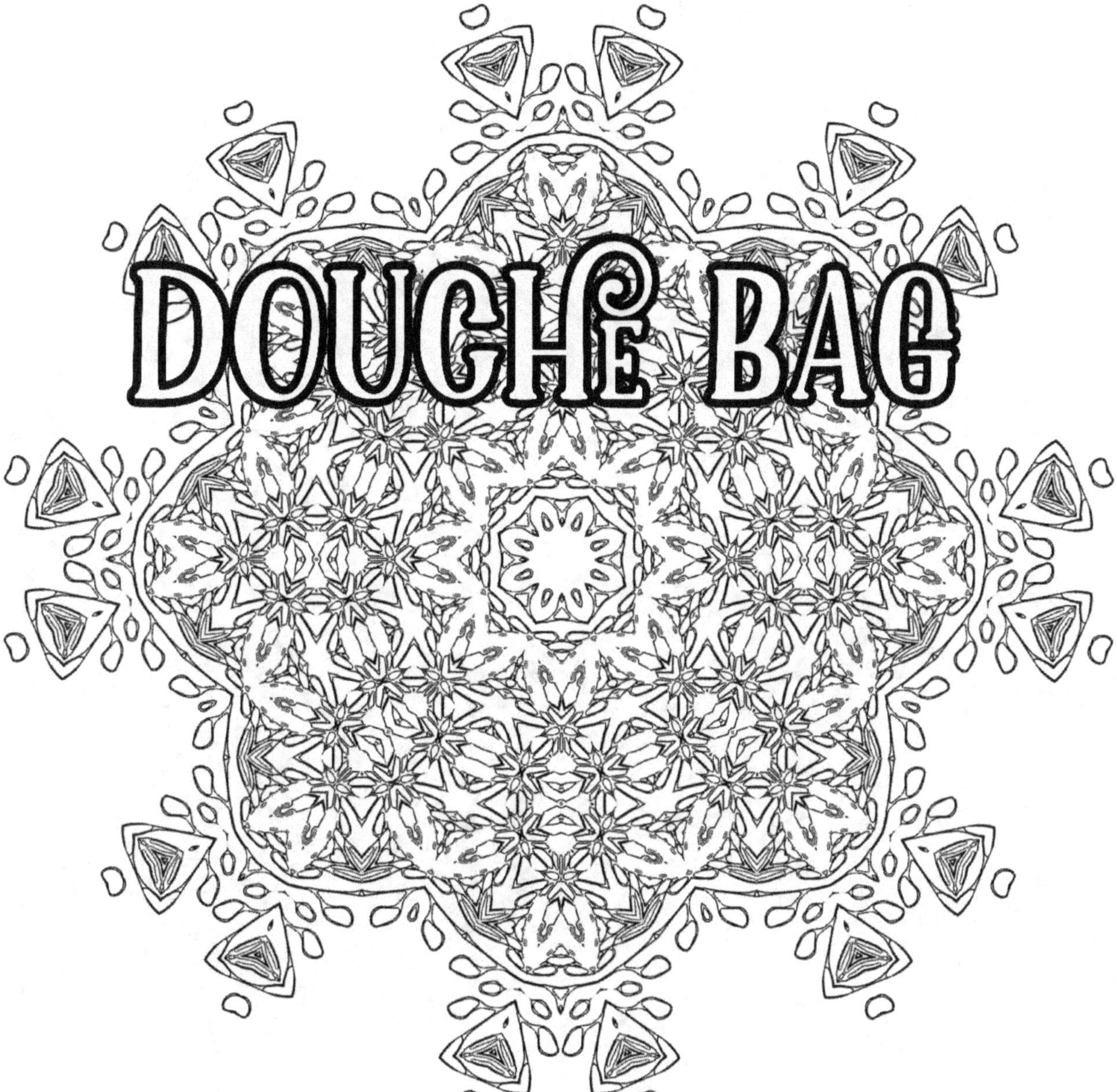
DOUCHE BAG

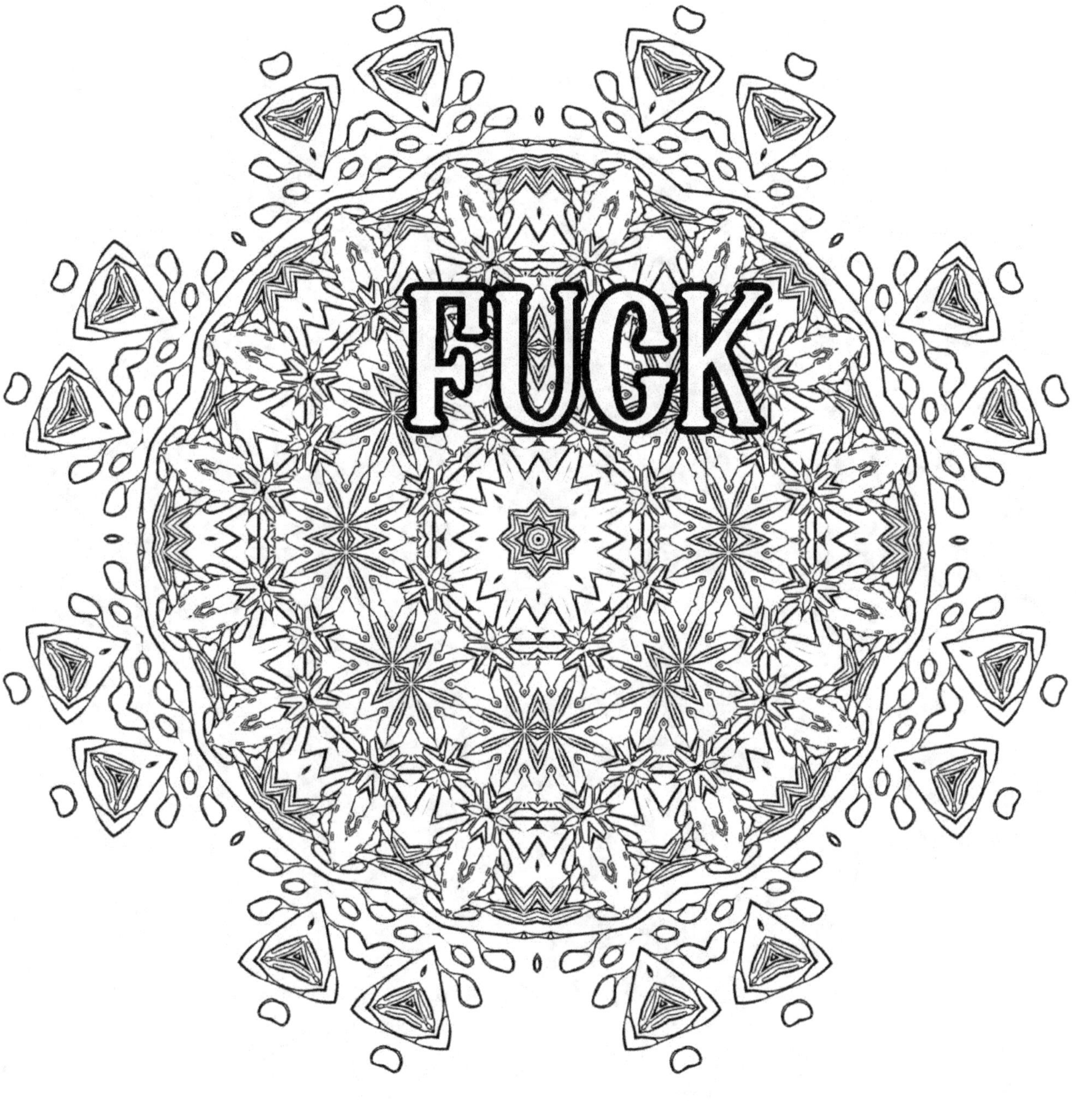
FUCK

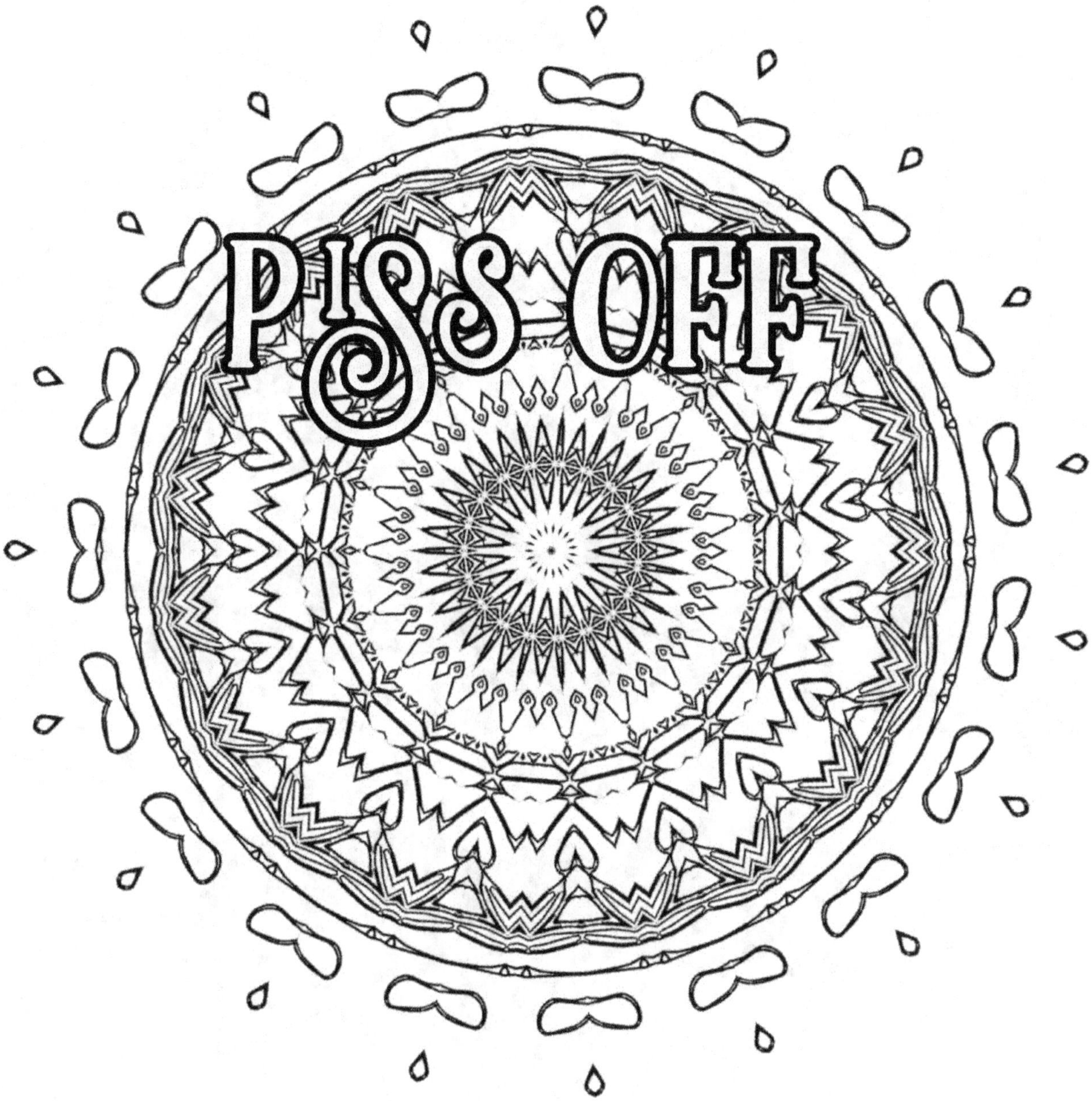
PISS OFF

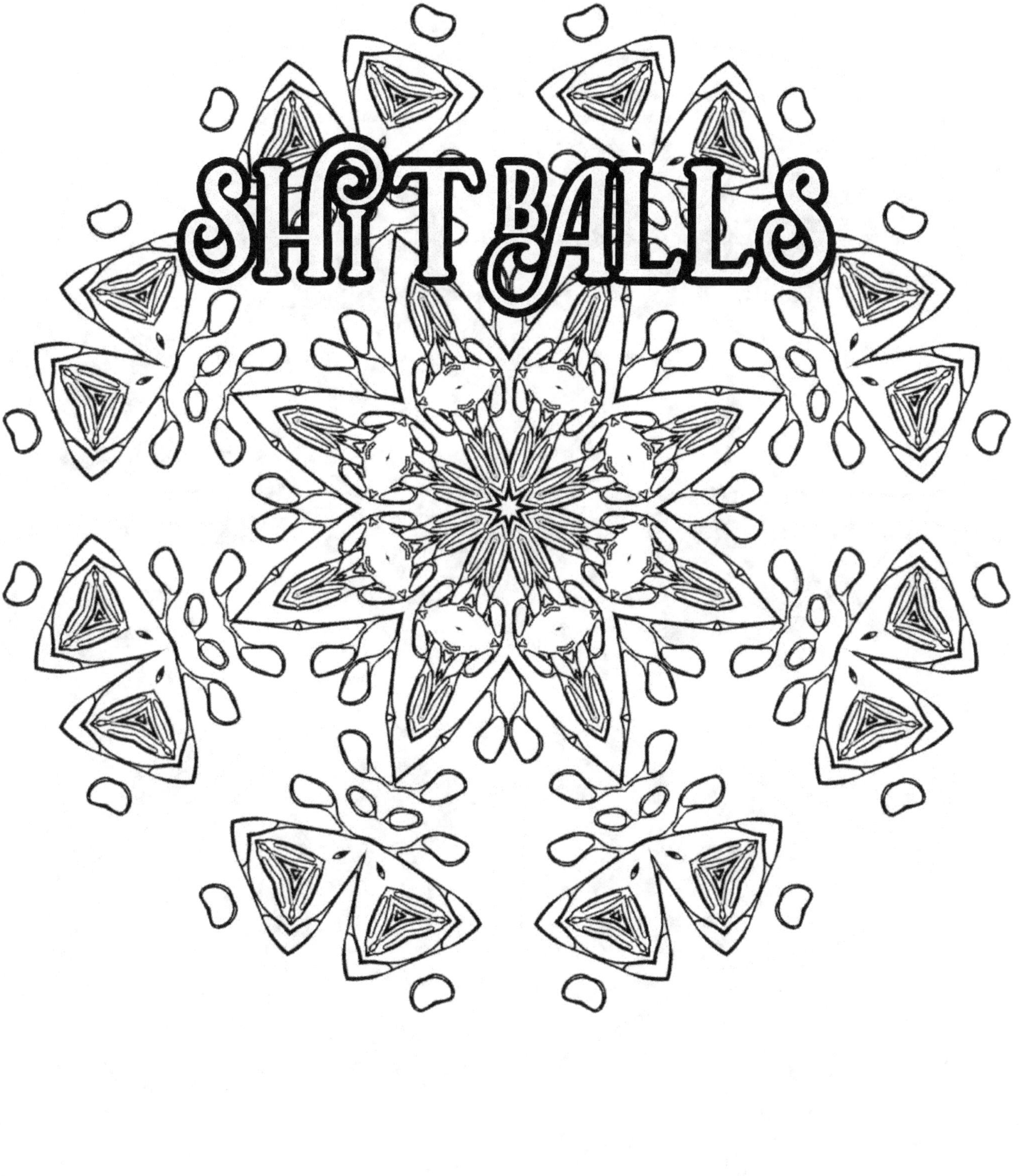
SHiT BALLS

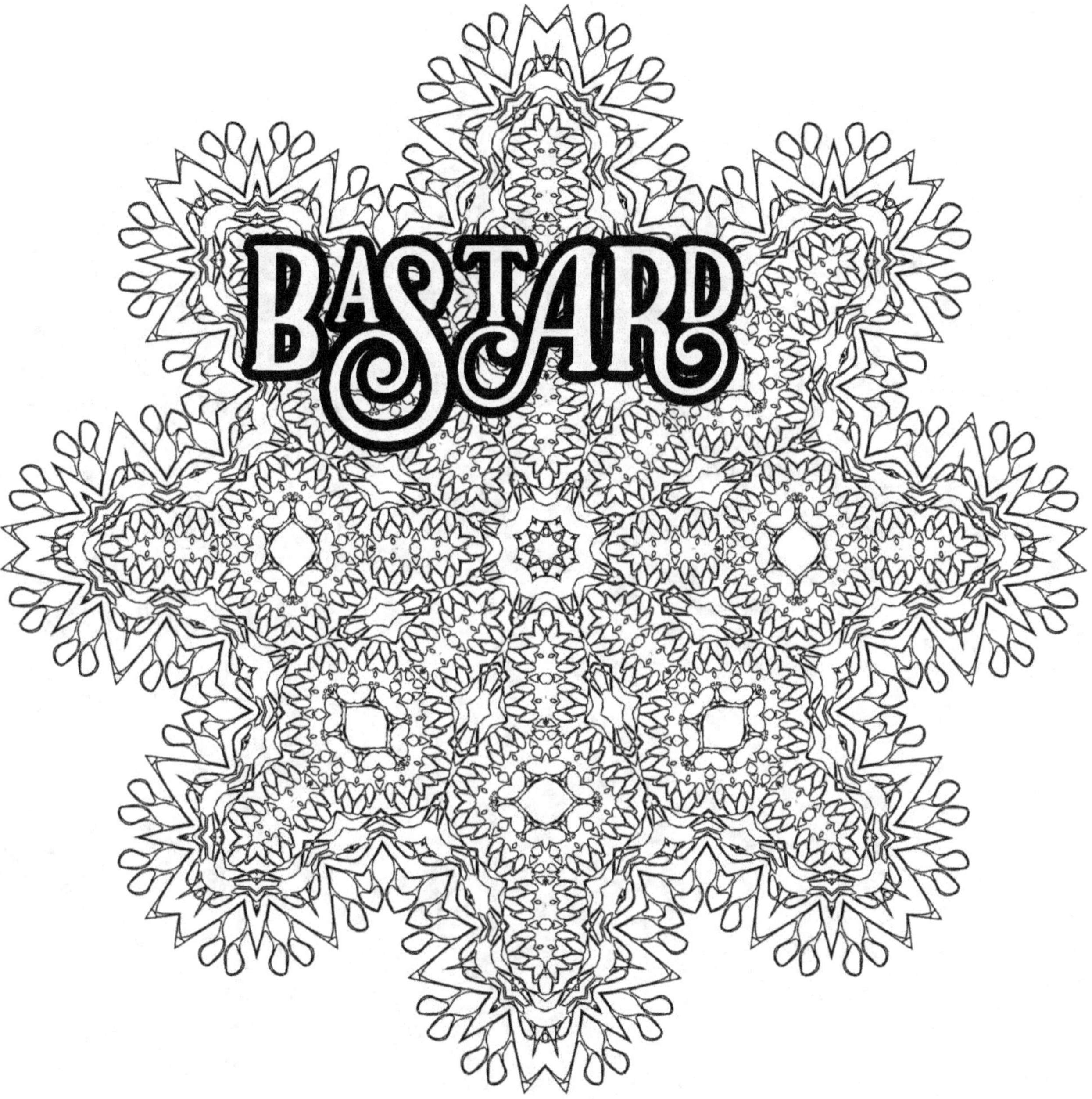
BASTARD

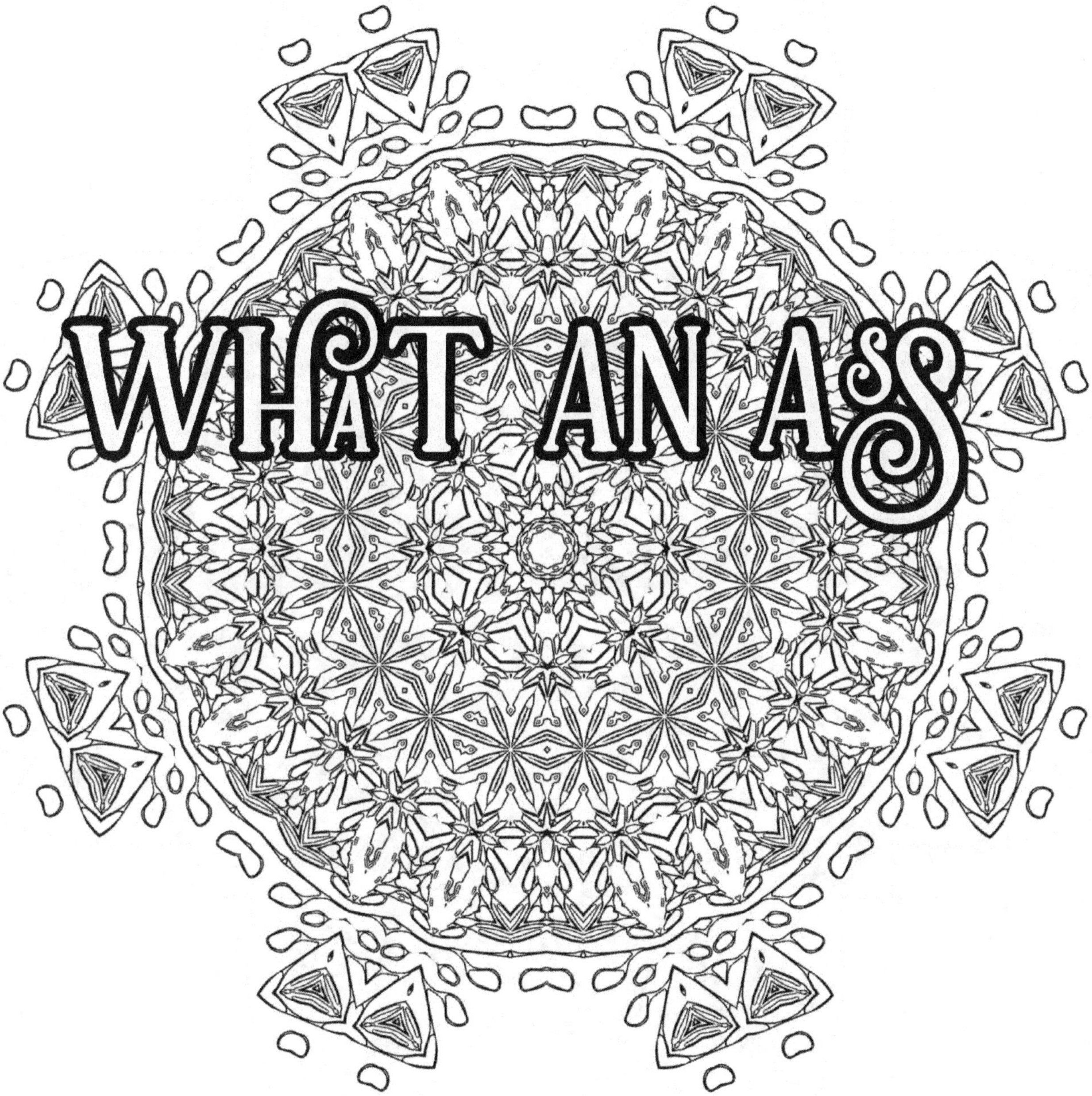
WHAT AN ASS

www.ingramcontent.com/pod-product-compliance
Lightning Source LLC
Chambersburg PA
CBHW081131180526
45170CB00008B/3068
9781544635958